POCAHONTAS

In 1607 the English come to Virginia. They want to begin a new life and to make their home in the New World. They build a town and call it Jamestown, after King James of England.

Virginia is a new world for the English, but it is not new for the Indian people of North America. They live there; their fathers and their grandfathers lived there before them. It is *their* country, *their* home. And they do not like these white men from across the sea.

One of the Englishmen, John Smith, goes up the river in a boat, but the Indians find him and take him to the great King, Powhatan. The Indians want to kill him, but Powhatan has a daughter—the beautiful Pocahontas. She looks into John Smith's blue, blue eyes … and so begins a famous story of two countries, two people, and a love without end.

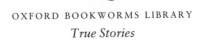

OXFORD BOOKWORMS LIBRARY

True Stories

Pocahontas

Stage 1 (400 headwords)

Series Editor: Jennifer Bassett
Founder Editor: Tricia Hedge
Activities Editors: Jennifer Bassett and Alison Baxter

American Edition: Daphne Mackey, University of Washington

RETOLD BY TIM VICARY

Pocahontas

Illustrated by
Thomas Sperling

OXFORD UNIVERSITY PRESS

ABE
F
F
VICARY

3 1257 02459 5117

OXFORD
UNIVERSITY PRESS

Great Clarendon Street, Oxford OX2 6DP

Oxford University Press is a department of the University of Oxford.
It furthers the University's objective of excellence in research, scholarship,
and education by publishing worldwide in

Oxford New York

Auckland Cape Town Dar es Salaam Hong Kong Karachi
Kuala Lumpur Madrid Melbourne Mexico City Nairobi
New Delhi Shanghai Taipei Toronto

With offices in

Argentina Austria Brazil Chile Czech Republic France Greece
Guatemala Hungary Italy Japan Poland Portugal Singapore
South Korea Switzerland Thailand Turkey Ukraine Vietnam

OXFORD and OXFORD ENGLISH are registered trade marks of
Oxford University Press in the UK and in certain other countries

This edition © Oxford University Press 2007

The moral rights of the author have been asserted.

Database right Oxford University Press (maker)

First published in Oxford Bookworms 1998

6 8 10 9 7

ISBN 978 0 19 423746 8

Printed in China

CONTENTS

STORY INTRODUCTION   i

1   The English in Virginia   1

2   John Smith and Pocahontas   8

3   A Friend for the English   15

4   A Wife for John Smith   20

5   Where Is John Smith?   24

6   A Husband for Pocahontas   29

7   England   34

GLOSSARY   42

ACTIVITIES: Before Reading   44

ACTIVITIES: While Reading   45

ACTIVITIES: After Reading   48

ABOUT THE AUTHOR   52

ABOUT THE BOOKWORMS LIBRARY   53

The English in Virginia

In January 1607 three ships left England and sailed to America. There were a hundred and fifty men on the ships, and they wanted to find a new world in the west— a home in a new and exciting country.

The ships were at sea for four months, and they arrived in Virginia on the 26th of April, 1607. After four long months at sea the men were tired, ill, and hungry. But Virginia was beautiful. The sky was blue, and they could see rivers, flowers, and forests of tall trees. The Englishmen were very happy.

They could see rivers, flowers, and forests.

1

But the Algonquin Indians of Virginia were not happy. They were afraid of the Englishmen and their ships. "This is our home," they said. "We don't want these white men here. We must fight them."

But some Indians said, "No, wait. These men are interesting. Let's make friends with them, and learn about them." So the Indians tried to talk to the Englishmen and gave them food to eat. The Englishmen gave things to the Indians, too—little knives, pictures, and beads.

The Englishmen gave the Indians pictures and beads.

The Englishmen began to build a little town. They called it Jamestown because the King of England was called James. They called the river James River, too.

The leaders of the Englishmen were Christopher Newport, Edward Wingfield, and John Smith. They wanted to learn more about Virginia, so Smith and Newport took twenty men and went up the river in a small boat.

The other men stayed in Jamestown with Wingfield. They began to build houses and to make gardens and fields outside the town.

"The fields are more important than the houses,"

They began to make fields outside the town.

said Wingfield. "And we must work quickly because it's nearly summer now. We must have corn and vegetables for the winter."

But it was not easy. The weather was hot, and the men were tired after four months at sea. Some men worked hard, but many sat in the sun and did nothing. The Indians watched and waited.

"We must have corn and vegetables for the winter."

3

Smith and Newport went thirty miles up the river. They visited Indian villages and talked to a lot of Indians. Some of the Indians were friendly, and some were not. When Smith and Newport came back to Jamestown, Wingfield was very pleased to see them.

"I was afraid for you," he said. "But you're not dead!"

"No, of course not," said Smith. "What's the matter?"

"It's the Indians," Wingfield said. "They're trying to kill us. Yesterday, they nearly killed *me*!"

"Well, what did you do?" Smith asked. "Our men have guns, and the Indians are very afraid of guns."

"But there were hundreds of Indians," said Wingfield, "and … we weren't ready. Our guns were on the ships."

"The men must carry their guns with them."

They moved the big guns from the ships onto the town walls.

"Why?" asked Smith angrily. "The men must always be ready; they must carry their guns with them. The Indians tried to kill you because they weren't afraid of you."

"Yes, but—we must be nice to them," said Wingfield.

"We can be friendly, but we must be careful first," said Smith. "We must build good walls around the town and put the big guns from the ships on them. Then the Indians can't kill us."

For a month everyone worked hard. They built walls around the town and moved the big guns from the ships.

But the men were afraid to work in the fields because of the Indians. And the sun got hotter and hotter.

In June Newport went back to England with two of the ships. A hundred and five men stayed in Jamestown. They had very little food. The corn from England was now bad, and the new corn in the fields was not ready. The river water was bad too, and soon many of the men were ill with a fever. Forty-six men died that summer.

Some of the men tried to leave Jamestown and go home in the ship, but Smith stopped them. "We're here to work and to build a new town," he said. "But first, we must find food. There are birds in the sky, fish in the river, animals in the forest—we must kill them and eat them. And we must get corn from the Indians, too. I can do that."

Smith wasn't afraid of the Indians, but he was always very careful. He carried his gun all the time. Most of the Indians were afraid of Smith, but they liked him too. He was friendly, and he loved their beautiful country. And he learned their language because he wanted to talk to them and understand them. Often, he gave the Indians little things from England, and they gave him food.

But when winter came, there were only fifty men alive in Jamestown. They had some food, but they needed more. The Virginian winter is long and cold, and fifty men need a lot of food.

"There are birds in the sky, fish in the river ..."

In December Smith went up the river in a boat with nine men. Two of the friendly Indians went with them. It was very cold, and the Englishmen were hungry. But Smith was happy and excited.

"I'm going to find food for Christmas," he said to the men in Jamestown. "Wait for me here, and work hard! This is a beautiful country, and we're going to stay here!"

John Smith and Pocahontas

There were a lot of Indian villages in Virginia, and every village had its Chief. But there was only one King. That was Powhatan, and he was the King of all the Algonquin Indians.

"Tell me about these white men," Powhatan said to his brother, Opekankanu. "They are living in my country and killing my people. I want to see one of them."

Powhatan's daughter, Pocahontas, heard this. She was thirteen years old. "What are white men, father?" she asked. "Are they white because they are ill?"

Powhatan smiled. "No, little Pocahontas, they aren't ill," he said. "They are a new people from over the sea. Perhaps we can see and talk to a white man soon. My brother is going to find one for us."

The next day Opekankanu went into the forest with two hundred men. They found John Smith's nine men next to their boat by the river. Smith's men were afraid and got out their guns. But Opekankanu's men killed two of them, and the other seven ran away.

John Smith was in the forest with the two Indians. When they heard the noise, they ran back to the boat— and saw two hundred men with bows and arrows. Then an arrow hit Smith's leg. He quickly took out his gun and put a friendly Indian in front of his body.

"What do you want?" he asked. "Don't come near me!"

"King Powhatan wants to see you," said Opekankanu. "Give me your gun."

An arrow hit Smith's leg.

"No," Smith said at first. But there were two hundred Indians, and he was one man. So he gave them his gun and went with Opekankanu to Werowocomoco, the village of King Powhatan.

In the village, everyone came out to see the Englishman. Pocahontas looked at Smith carefully. He was very interesting. He was not very tall, and he had hair on his face. Indian men had no hair on their faces. And his eyes—his eyes were blue! All the men in her village had brown eyes. She looked at Smith's blue eyes for a long time. They were beautiful, the color of the sky.

Smith smiled at the little girl and closed one of his eyes for a second. Pocahontas laughed, and then she smiled back at him.

"Why are you in my country, white man?" Powhatan asked. "Where do you come from? Who is your King?"

Smith told him about England, King James, and Jamestown. It wasn't easy because he didn't understand Powhatan's language very well, and Powhatan didn't always understand him. "We want to live here and be your friends, Powhatan," he said. "But this winter the people of Jamestown are hungry, so we need food."

Opekankanu was angry. "These Englishmen cannot live here," he said to his brother. "They are taking our land and killing our people with their guns. They want

"Why are you in my country, white man?"

King James of England to be king here, too. They call their town *King James's town*, and they call our beautiful river *King James's river*! But what about us? This is *our* country! We live here, and our fathers and grandfathers lived here before us. We don't want the English, or their King James. We must kill them all now!"

"Perhaps," Powhatan said. "But let's think first. The

11

English have guns, so we need guns too. I must think carefully about this. Pocahontas, come with me."

They walked into the forest, and Powhatan asked his daughter, "What do you think about this Englishman, little Pocahontas?"

"Oh, father, I like him. He has wonderful blue eyes—the color of the sky."

"My brother wants to kill him, but I want to know more about these Englishmen first—and you can help me. I'm going to give him to you, little Pocahontas."

"Give him to me, father?"

"Yes. Listen carefully, now. You must do this …"

They went back to the village. "Are we going to kill this white man now, Powhatan?" Opekankanu asked.

"Yes," Powhatan said. "Bring him here."

They put John Smith's head on a stone in front of Powhatan's feet. Then Opekankanu took a big stick and walked to the stone. Pocahontas looked at her father. He moved his head a little, but did not look at her. Now Opekankanu was next to the stone. John Smith closed his eyes and waited to die.

Suddenly, he felt warm arms on his face and head. He

Suddenly, Smith felt warm arms on his face and head.

13

opened his eyes and saw the face of the young girl with her beautiful dark eyes.

"No, Opekankanu!" she cried. "No! I am the King's daughter, and I say no!" She looked at her father. "Father—don't kill this man—please! Give him to me!"

At first Powhatan said nothing. Then, slowly, he smiled. "Very well, Pocahontas," he said. "You are only thirteen years old, but this white man is not very big. He is a boy with hair on his face. You can have him."

Angrily, Opekankanu put his stick down.

Pocahontas smiled. "Come with me, white man," she said to him. "You are my Englishman now. Come!"

"Come with me, white man," Pocahontas said.

A Friend for the English

John Smith stayed with Pocahontas for some days. She learned some English, and he learned more of her language. Soon they were good friends.

But Powhatan's men watched Smith carefully, and he could not leave the village. Then one day Powhatan said, "You can go home to Jamestown, John Smith. But you must give me two of your big guns."

John Smith did not like this, but he could not say no. So he went back to Jamestown, and Pocahontas, Opekankanu, and some Indians went with him.

In Jamestown Wingfield was not happy. "We can't give our big guns to the Indians!" he said. "Then they can kill us, with *our* guns!"

"It's all right," said Smith. "Wait."

He took Opekankanu and his men to the guns on the town walls. "Now watch," he said. He put some gunpowder and some stones in the gun. "Put your hands over your ears," he said, "and look at that tree."

BANG! Pocahontas closed her eyes. Then she opened them and looked at the tree. It wasn't there!

"What happened?" she asked. "Where's the tree?"

"I killed it with this gun," Smith said. He looked at

The tree wasn't there!

Opekankanu. "This gun can kill ten men, Opekankanu. Remember that. So, take your two guns."

But the guns were very big, and of course, the Indians could not move them.

"Look," said Smith. "You can't carry these guns

through the forest. But I can give you some gunpowder for Powhatan. Here, take it. Be very careful with it."

"Thank you," Opekankanu said. "But one day, we want these big guns too. They are very important for us."

"Perhaps," said Smith. "But we want to be your friends, and friends are better than guns."

❋   ❋   ❋

That winter, Pocahontas came to Jamestown every week with food for the Englishmen. She learned many interesting things in Jamestown.

"Look at this, Pocahontas," John Smith said one day. He had a compass in his hand.

"What is it?" Pocahontas asked. She tried to put her finger on the arrow in the compass, but she couldn't.

Smith had a compass in his hand.

17

"It's a compass. The arrow always points to the north," Smith said. "Where is the north? Do you know?"

"Of course I know. All my people know that."

"Well, look—the arrow in the compass knows it too!"

"Why can't I put my finger on it?"

Smith smiled. "Because of the glass. You can see through glass, but you can't put your finger through it."

"Yes," she said slowly. "But—what is a compass for?"

"It helps us in our ships when we can't see the sky," he said. "Which way do we go? Where is the north? The compass tells us all that."

Pocahontas was interested in everything. She loved to talk to John Smith, and she learned many things about England and the English.

❋   ❋   ❋

In March and April 1608, two more ships came to Jamestown. Powhatan asked Pocahontas about them.

"How many Englishmen are there now?" he asked.

"There were thirty-eight before the ships came, father. But now there are about a hundred and fifty."

"It's spring now. They must sow corn and vegetables in their fields. Are they doing that?"

"Yes, father. But they aren't very good at it. This is a new country for them. They don't understand it."

"But they must have corn!" Powhatan was angry. "They need food for the winter. We can't give them our corn every year! And we kill animals, birds, and fish for our food—the English must learn to do that too!"

"They *are* learning, father," Pocahontas said. "But most of these men come from towns in England. They don't know about these things."

"Well, they live here now, so they must learn," said Powhatan. "Or they must give me guns. We have a lot of food in our village, but we need guns. I can give the Englishmen food, but they must give me guns first. Tell that to your English friends, Pocahontas!"

"Tell that to your English friends, Pocahontas!"

19

A Wife for 4 John Smith

But the English didn't want to give Powhatan any guns. "Oh no, Pocahontas," John Smith said. "Your father has thousands of men, but we have only a hundred and fifty. We can't give him guns."

Later, some of Powhatan's men tried to take guns from the English. Smith was very angry. He locked the men in a little room in Jamestown for a week. Then he talked to Pocahontas about them.

Smith locked the men in a little room in Jamestown.

"This world is a big round ball, too."

"I'm very angry with these men, Pocahontas," he said. "But I'm not going to kill them because your father didn't kill me in Werowocomoco. I'm going to give them to you. Take them home, Pocahontas."

Pocahontas liked the English, and she often visited Jamestown. John Smith liked to teach her new things.

"The sun, Pocahontas," he said one evening, "is a red ball in the sky. This world is a big round ball, too. Thirty years ago, an Englishman called Francis Drake sailed around the world in a ship."

Pocahontas laughed. "But that's not true! Of course the world isn't a ball! Why does the sea stay on it, then?"

Smith smiled. "Oh, I can tell you. Listen …"

He talked well, so it was easy to understand him.

Pocahontas listened and watched his beautiful blue eyes. She was fourteen years old, and for her, John Smith was the most exciting man in the world.

"Do you have a wife, John Smith?" she asked one day.

"No," he said slowly. "Why do you ask?"

"Oh, because one day I must have a husband, and ..." She did not finish, but John Smith understood.

"Pocahontas," he said carefully, "you are only fourteen years old, and I'm twenty-eight. And the daughter of the King must marry somebody important."

"You *are* an important man in Jamestown," she said quickly. "And my people and your people must learn to be friends. A husband and wife can ..."

"Stop." He put his finger on her mouth. "Pocahontas, I like you very much, but I'm not the right husband for you, and ... I don't know a lot about women."

"I can teach you about that!" she said.

He looked at her in surprise and laughed. She was angry when he laughed.

"I'm nearly fifteen. In my village a girl can have a husband when she is fifteen! Why are you laughing?"

"I'm sorry," he said. "You are a beautiful, interesting girl, Pocahontas. But you are only a child!"

"I'm not a child! You're afraid of me, because I'm a King's daughter, and I want you for my husband."

Pocahontas was angry and unhappy. She went away,

"You are only a child!" said John Smith.

back to her father's village, and she didn't visit John Smith again for two months. But she thought about him every day. There was only one man in the world for Pocahontas, and that was John Smith.

And in Jamestown, perhaps John Smith thought about Pocahontas, too.

Where Is John Smith?

In the winter of 1608 the English in Jamestown were hungry again. So John Smith went to Werowocomoco and asked Powhatan for corn. He took many beautiful glass beads with him, because the Indians loved these things. But Powhatan wanted more than beads.

"You can have corn," he said, "but you must build one of your big English houses for me—with windows of glass. And you must give me some guns."

"A house—yes," said Smith. "Tomorrow my men can bring things from Jamestown and begin to build a house for you. But guns—no. Friends do not need guns."

Powhatan smiled, but he was angry, very angry. "Yes, we are friends," he said. "Tonight you must stay here and eat with us. Tomorrow you can have your corn."

That night Pocahontas came to John Smith. She was afraid. "My father is angry," she said. "He wants to kill you and all your men. You must be careful!"

John Smith took her hands. "What a good friend you are, Pocahontas!" he said. "How can I thank you?"

Pocahontas looked into his blue eyes. "You are my King," she said quietly. "My King—now, and always."

So Smith and his men carried their guns all the time,

and they watched very carefully. The next morning Opekankanu and his women came with the corn.

"There is your corn," Opekankanu said. "Now, give us your guns!" He smiled. "Look behind you!"

Smith looked. And seven hundred Indians came out of the forest with bows and arrows.

"Look behind you!" said Opekankanu.

In a second, John Smith had his gun in Opekankanu's face.

How can ten men fight seven hundred? In a second, John Smith had his hand in Opekankanu's hair and his gun in Opekankanu's face.

"My gun can kill *you*," he said angrily, "before an arrow can get to *me*." He looked at Opekankanu's men. "Do you want Opekankanu to die?" he called.

The Indians were afraid of John Smith. To them, he was a King, and it is not easy to kill a King. They put down their bows and arrows and went away into the forest. Opekankanu, too, was afraid. His women put the corn in Smith's boat, and Smith and his men went back down the river to Jamestown.

Powhatan and Opekankanu were angry. "We don't want these Englishmen in our country," Powhatan said. "We must kill them—kill them all!"

"No, father!" said Pocahontas. "We must learn to be friends with the English. John Smith says—"

"Be quiet!" Powhatan said. "John Smith is our enemy. Stay away from him! Do you understand?"

"But you gave him to me, father. Do you remember? I loved his blue eyes then, and I love them now. I cannot stay away from him."

Pocahontas did visit John Smith after that, but not very often. It wasn't easy for her. There was often fighting between the English and the Indians now, and dead men do not make friends.

More ships and more men came from England—and more guns. Jamestown was now a town of five hundred people—five hundred hungry people. The English wanted the Indians' corn, and the Indians wanted the Englishmen's guns.

One day, in October 1609, Pocahontas went to Jamestown, but she could not find John Smith.

"Where is he?" she asked some Englishmen.

"Smith? He left Jamestown a month ago," one man said. "He had a bad accident with some gunpowder. He was very ill. So he went home to England."

"Ill?" Pocahontas said. "John Smith is ill?"

"Yes," the man said. "It was a very bad accident. And six weeks on a ship ... perhaps he's dead now."

"Did—did he leave a letter for me?" Pocahontas asked.

The man laughed. "A letter for you, little girl? But you can't read! Why? Is it important?"

"No," she said. "It's not important." But of course it was.

She went away into the forest and cried for a long time. Where was John Smith, her Englishman with blue eyes, the color of the sky?

Pocahontas went away into the forest and cried for a long time.

A Husband for Pocahontas

For four years after that, things were very bad. Sometimes Pocahontas tried to help the English. But to Powhatan and Opekankanu, the English were enemies, and they wanted to kill them all.

Powhatan gave the English no more corn. His men came at night to Jamestown and took guns and other things. When they found Englishmen in the forest or by the river, they killed them and took their guns. And so Powhatan now had many guns in Werowocomoco.

The new leaders of Jamestown were very unhappy about this. "How can we stop Powhatan?" they said. "We must get those guns back from him."

"We need to take a hostage," said a man called Samuel Argall. "One of the Chiefs, or somebody important from Powhatan's family. Then we can talk to Powhatan. We can give him back the hostage when he gives us the guns—but not before."

"Powhatan has a daughter, Pocahontas," said an older man. "He loves her very much, they say ..."

※　※　※

In 1613 Pocahontas was nineteen. She lived now with her father's friend, Iapassus, and his wife. Iapassus was

"You must come with me to Jamestown," said Argall.

friendly with the English, and so it was easy for Samuel Argall. He came to Iapassus' village in his ship.

"I have many beautiful things from England in my ship," he told Iapassus. "They are all for you—but first, you must give *me* something. You must bring Pocahontas onto my ship and leave her here."

So Iapassus took Pocahontas onto the ship, and Argall locked her in a room. Pocahontas was very angry.

"I'm sorry," Argall said to her, "but you must come with me to Jamestown. Your father must stop fighting us, and he must give us back our guns. Then you can go home."

So Pocahontas went to Jamestown and stayed there. At first, Powhatan was angry. He wanted his daughter.

But then he looked at his guns, and he wanted them more than his daughter.

"We can kill the English with these guns," he said to Opekankanu. "Pocahontas likes the English. She can stay in Jamestown—and the guns can stay here."

❋   ❋   ❋

There were many women in Jamestown now, and Pocahontas soon made new friends. The Englishwomen liked her very much. She stayed in their houses, played with their children, and spoke English all the time.

After some months, one of her new friends asked her,

The Englishwomen liked Pocahontas very much.

"Are you happy here with us, Pocahontas? Would you like to go home to your people?"

"The English are my people now," said Pocahontas.

"But perhaps one day your father—" said her friend.

"My father," said Pocahontas, "likes his guns better than his daughter. They are more important to him. This is my home now, and I am very happy here."

One of her new friends was a man called John Rolfe. Pocahontas liked him. Rolfe was a tall man, with brown eyes. He liked Pocahontas, too, and visited her nearly every day. He smiled a lot and often laughed happily.

One day he said, "Pocahontas, I have something important to say to you. We are good friends, I think, and … well, we can be more than friends. I need a wife, Pocahontas, and—you are the most beautiful woman in Jamestown. And the most interesting woman, too! I love you, Pocahontas, and I want to marry you."

At first Pocahontas didn't say anything. John Rolfe was a nice man, but a long time ago, she remembered, she wanted to be the wife of a different John. "But I'm never going to see John Smith again," she thought. "He's dead. I must forget about him."

She smiled at John Rolfe. "Yes, John," she said. "I would very much like to be your wife."

And so, on the 5th of April, 1614, an Indian girl married an Englishman in the church in Jamestown.

Pocahontas' father did not come, but Opekankanu was there, with many of her people.

"Your father is happy for you," Opekankanu told her.

Pocahontas was happy, too. John Rolfe was a good husband, and a year later, they had a little son, Thomas. Pocahontas loved him very much.

Pocahontas married John Rolfe in the church in Jamestown.

33

England

In 1616, Pocahontas, John Rolfe, and their son went to England. Ten of her people came too. After seven weeks on the ship, they arrived in London.

"How big London is!" Pocahontas said. "There are hundreds of houses here—and thousands of people!"

London was very noisy and exciting. Pocahontas was

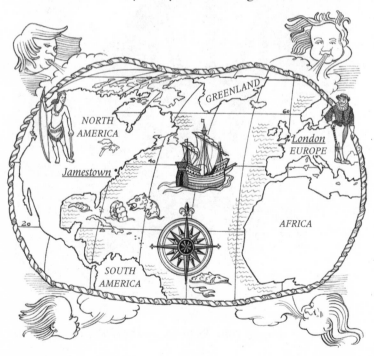

London was very noisy and exciting.

interested in everything. She went into the shops and
looked at the food, the dresses, and the books. She
went up and down the River Thames in a boat and saw
the big houses of rich people. Every day, she saw
something new and wonderful.

But London was very dirty, too, because there were so
many people. The river was dirty, and the water was
bad. Two of Pocahontas' people were ill and died.

But Pocahontas was happy and excited. Every day she
visited big houses and talked to rich and important
people. Everybody in London wanted to meet her, to
talk to her, and to be her friend.

The King and Queen of England heard about John Rolfe's wife, the Indian girl from Virginia, and they wanted to meet her, too. So one day Pocahontas went to visit King James and Queen Anne. They asked her about her father, Powhatan.

"My father is the King of the Algonquin people," she said. "He has many men and villages. But our country is quieter than England. Our people understand the forest, the animals, and the rivers. You can learn from us, and we can learn from you, too. We must be friends."

One day Pocahontas went to visit King James and Queen Anne.

36

"Of course we must," King James said. "Jamestown has my name, so I'm very interested in it."

They talked for some time, and then his wife, Queen Anne, said, "I have a letter about you, Pocahontas. It's from a man called John Smith. He was your friend, he says, when you were a little girl. Is that true?"

For a second or two Pocahontas could not speak. Then she said, "A letter from John Smith? But he's dead!"

Queen Anne smiled. "Dead? No, he's here in England. Look, here is the letter." The Queen looked at Pocahontas. "What's the matter, my dear? Are you ill?"

"No, no, I'm all right. I'm very happy."

But that night, Pocahontas could not sleep. She was very excited. John Smith was not dead. He was alive, and in England! But where?

Two days later, John Smith came to see her.

He was older, of course. But she remembered him. A little man, not tall, but interesting, exciting, and alive. He smiled at her, with those beautiful blue eyes. "Hello, Pocahontas," he said. "Do you remember me?"

How could she forget him? She looked at him, but said nothing. John Rolfe watched them. "It's John Smith, my dear," he said. "Are you happy to see him?"

But Pocahontas was not happy. "No," she said. "I'm sorry. *No.*" She looked out of the window, at nothing. She couldn't look at John Smith.

37

"Hello, Pocahontas. Do you remember me?"

John Rolfe went out, and Smith waited. After a
minute he said, "You are a wife now and a mother."

"Yes." Pocahontas looked at him and tried to smile.

"Do I look different?" he asked. "I'm older, I know."

"No, you don't look different," she said. "But—why
did you go away from Virginia?"

"I had an accident," he said. "I was very ill. So I came
back to England, and after two years I got better."

"In Jamestown they told me you were dead."

"Dead? No, not me."

"But you didn't tell me! You didn't write me a letter—not one letter in eight years, John Smith!"

"But you were a child, Pocahontas. You couldn't read!"

"Well, I can read now!" she said angrily. "Perhaps I *was* a child, John Smith, but my father gave you to me—that day in my father's village long ago. Do you remember? That day was the beginning of my love for you."

He looked at her sadly with those beautiful blue eyes, and she was a child again. She remembered everything.

"You didn't love me," she said. "You never loved me."

"I … don't know about love," he said slowly. "You are the daughter of a King, Pocahontas, and I'm not rich or important. I never had a wife; perhaps I don't understand women. And you were a child, Pocahontas."

"I was a child—but I loved you, and you went away," she said. "For eight years I heard nothing from you."

For a long time he said nothing. Then he said. "I'm sorry, Pocahontas. I was wrong."

"I loved you so much," she said sadly. Then the door opened, and her little son, Thomas, came in. "But now I have a son and a husband," she said. "And they love me. You and I cannot be friends. Goodbye, John Smith."

"Goodbye, Pocahontas." He looked at her for a

minute, and then walked out of the door. She never saw him again.

Six months later, John Rolfe said, "We must go back to Virginia, my dear. My work is waiting for me there. And you need the warm sun of Virginia, too."

It was true. Pocahontas was now ill, and the cold rain of the English winter was not good for her. But she said

"Goodbye, John. I am going home …"

40

nothing and got ready to leave. The ship went down the river from London to a town called Gravesend, near the sea. But when they got there, Pocahontas was very ill, and she could not move. John Rolfe sat by his wife's bed and watched her face sadly.

She smiled at him. "Goodbye, John. I am going home—home to the forests and rivers of my country."

❈ ❈ ❈

Pocahontas died in Gravesend in March 1617.

She is famous for two things. She was the first American woman to marry an Englishman and come to England. And she was a good friend to the English when they first went to Virginia.

Her husband, John Rolfe, went back to Virginia and married an Englishwoman there. He died in Virginia in 1622. Pocahontas' son, Thomas, lived with the Rolfe family in England when he was a child, but in 1635 he went to live in Virginia.

John Smith did not leave England again. He wrote many interesting books about America, and he wrote about Pocahontas in those books. He lived until 1631, but he never had a wife. Perhaps he could not forget the sad, dark eyes of Pocahontas, when she said goodbye to him for the last time.

GLOSSARY

build to make buildings (houses, schools, shops, etc.)

chief the most important man in an Indian village

enemy not a friend; a person who hates you

fever when you are ill with a very hot head and body, you have a fever

fight to hit, hurt, or try to kill someone

glass bottles and windows are made of glass

gunpowder a powder used in guns that burns very quickly

hard a lot (e.g., to work hard)

hostage your enemy takes somebody as a hostage because he wants something from you

king the most important man in a country

leader an important person in a group of people

lock (*v*) to close (a door, box, etc.) with a key

marry to take somebody as your husband or wife

queen the wife of a king

sadly not happily

sail to go over water (the sea, rivers, etc.) in a ship

sow to put small plants in the ground

surprise when something new or sudden happens, you feel surprise

try to work hard to do something

unhappy not happy

Pocahontas

ACTIVITIES

ACTIVITIES

Before Reading

1 **Read the story introduction on the first page of the book and the back cover. Are these sentences true? Check one box for each sentence.**

	YES	NO
1 Pocahontas has blue eyes.	☐	☐
2 Pocahontas is the daughter of a king.	☐	☐
3 The English came to Virginia for a holiday.	☐	☐
4 The English call their town after their king.	☐	☐
5 The Indians lived in North America for a long time before 1607.	☐	☐
6 The Indians wanted the English to go home.	☐	☐
7 Pocahontas meets John Smith in Jamestown.	☐	☐

2 **What happens in this story? Can you guess? Choose words to complete these sentences.**

1 Pocahontas marries *John Smith / another Englishman.*

2 The Indians *kill /don't kill* John Smith.

3 The English and the Indians are *enemies / good friends.*

4 John Smith *stays in Virginia / goes back to England.*

5 Pocahontas *stays in Virginia / visits England.*

6 *Pocahontas / John Smith* dies when *she / he* is still young.

7 The story has *a happy / an unhappy* ending.

ACTIVITIES

While Reading

Read Chapter 1. How many true sentences can you make from this table?

The Indians The Englishmen	had wanted built	a town. knives. houses. corn. ships. guns. beads. pictures.

Read Chapters 2 and 3. Who said these words, and to whom?

1 "They are a new people from over the sea."
2 "We want to live here and be your friends."
3 "We don't want the English, or their King James."
4 "He has wonderful blue eyes—the color of the sky."
5 "I am the King's daughter, and I say no!"
6 "One day, we want these big guns too."
7 ". . . friends are better than guns."
8 "We can't give them our corn every year!"

Before you read Chapter 4, can you guess what happens?

1 Do the Englishmen give any guns to Powhatan?
2 What happens between Pocahontas and John Smith?

Read Chapter 4. Here are some untrue sentences about it. Change them into true sentences.

1 The Englishmen had thousands of men.
2 Pocahontas never visited Jamestown.
3 Pocahontas taught John Smith many new things.
4 To Pocahontas, John Smith was the richest man in the world.
5 Pocahontas wanted John Smith for her friend.
6 Pocahontas didn't think about John Smith for two months.

Read Chapter 5 and answer these questions.

1 What did Powhatan want from John Smith?
2 How did Powhatan feel about John Smith's answer?
3 Where did the seven hundred Indians come from?
4 Why did the Indians put down their bows and arrows?
5 Why was it difficult for Pocahontas to visit John Smith?
6 What did the Englishmen and the Indians want?
7 How many people now lived in Jamestown?
8 Why did John Smith go home to England?
9 What did Pocahontas do when she left Jamestown?

Before you read Chapter 6, can you guess what happens? Choose one of these answers.

Pocahontas marries ...
1 John Smith.   2 another Englishman.   3 an Indian.

Read Chapter 6. Choose the best question-word for these questions, and then answer them.

Why / *Who* / *What*
1 ... did the Indians do to the Englishmen?
2 ... did the English take a hostage?
3 ... did Powhatan want more—his guns or his daughter?
4 ... did Pocahontas make friends with?
5 ... wanted to marry Pocahontas?
6 ... did he want to marry her?

Read Chapter 7. Are these sentences true (T) or false (F)? Change the false sentences into true ones.

1 Pocahontas was interested in everything in London.
2 Nobody in London wanted to be Pocahontas' friend.
3 Queen Anne told Pocahontas that John Smith was dead.
4 Pocahontas was a child when John Smith went away.
5 She was happy when John Smith came to see her.
6 The cold weather in England was bad for Pocahontas.
7 Pocahontas died when she was an old woman.
8 John Smith never went to North America again.

After Reading

1 **What did Powhatan say to Pocahontas in the forest? Put their conversation in the right order, and write in the speakers' names. Powhatan speaks first (number 3).**

1 _____ "Run to John Smith and put your arms over his head, before Opekankanu's stick comes down."

2 _____ "Yes, I can. But *why* must I do this, father? You are the King. *You* can say 'no' to Opekankanu."

3 _____ "Listen, Pocahontas. When the men bring the Englishman in front of me and put his head on the stone, you must watch Opekankanu."

4 _____ "And then do I take John Smith away?"

5 _____ "Of course I can say 'no.' But I want John Smith to learn something."

6 _____ "Run? Run where, father?"

7 _____ "He must learn that I am the King in this country. And a King can give life, or he can take it away."

8 _____ "Do I speak to Opekankanu?"

9 _____ "No, first you must ask for his life. Say, 'Father— don't kill this man!' Can you do this for me?"

10 _____ "Learn what, father?"

11 _____ "No, say nothing. Just watch him. But when he walks to the stone with his stick, get ready to run."

2 Find these words in the word search below, and draw a line through them. The words go from left to right, and from top to bottom.

arrow, bead, bird, bow, chief, church, compass, corn, field, finger, fish, glass, gun, queen, stone, vegetables, walls, world

C	O	R	N	M	Y	F	F	A	T	H	W
O	E	R	L	I	F	I	E	L	D	C	O
M	K	G	L	A	S	S	C	E	S	H	R
P	H	I	B	S	G	H	H	U	N	U	L
A	R	R	O	W	S	B	I	B	I	R	D
S	S	E	W	A	Q	U	E	E	N	C	T
S	T	T	E	L	R	T	F	A	H	H	A
N	O	H	I	L	S	D	A	D	G	U	N
U	N	G	H	S	T	F	I	N	G	E	R
V	E	G	E	T	A	B	L	E	S	E	R

Now write down all the letters without a line through them. Begin with the first line, and go across each line to the end. There are 41 letters, and they make a sentence of 9 words.

1 What is the sentence?

2 Who said it in the story?

3 Where was the speaker at the time?

4 How was the speaker's life different now?

3 Here is a new illustration for the story. Find the best place in the story to put the picture, and answer these questions.

The picture goes on page ____.

1 Who are the people in the picture?
2 Where are they—in which city and which country?
3 Why is the woman sad?

Now write a caption for the illustration.

Caption: _____

4 Here is John Smith's letter to King James and Queen Anne. Circle the correct words.

Dear King James and Queen Anne,

My friends *tell* / *say* me that Pocahontas is *in* / *at* London. I *do* / *would* like to see *him* / *her* very much. We *were* / *are* friends in Virginia. Her *brother's father* / *father's brother* wanted to *kill* / *die* me, but Pocahontas *stopped* / *made* him. She *usually* / *often* came to Jamestown, and she helped the English *a lot* / *a little* in those early days. She was a *big* / *little* girl then. Does she *remember* / *forget* me now? Perhaps I *can* / *must* see her in London. Please tell her about *us* / *me* and say *goodbye* / *hello* to her from me.

John Smith

5 What did you think about the people in this story? Did you like them? Did you feel sorry for anybody? Choose some names, and complete some of these sentences.

Pocahontas / *John Smith* / *Powhatan* / *John Rolfe* / *Opekankanu* / *Samuel Argall*

1 I liked _____ because _____.
2 I didn't like _____ because _____.
3 I felt sorry for _____ when _____.
4 _____ was right to _____.
5 _____ was wrong to _____.
6 I was angry with _____ when _____.

ABOUT THE AUTHOR

Tim Vicary is an experienced teacher and writer and has written several stories for the Oxford Bookworms Library. Many of these are in the Thriller & Adventure series, such as *White Death* (at Stage 1), or in the True Stories series, such as *The Coldest Place on Earth* (also at Stage 1), which tells the story of Scott's and Amundsen's race to the South Pole.

All the characters in this story about Pocahontas were real people. Tim Vicary used John Smith's own book, *A General History of Virginia*, which John Smith wrote in 1626, some years after Pocahontas died. The story of Pocahontas is also told in a famous Disney film, but it is a very different story from the one in John Smith's book.

Tim Vicary has two children, and keeps dogs, cats, and horses. He lives and works in York, in the north of England, and has also published two long novels, *The Blood upon the Rose* and *Cat and Mouse*.

OXFORD BOOKWORMS LIBRARY

Classics • Crime & Mystery • Factfiles • Fantasy & Horror
Human Interest • Playscripts • Thriller & Adventure
True Stories • World Stories

The OXFORD BOOKWORMS LIBRARY provides enjoyable reading in English, with a wide range of classic and modern fiction, non-fiction, and plays. It includes original and adapted texts in seven carefully graded language stages which take learners from beginner to advanced level.

All Stage 1 titles, as well as over eighty other titles from Starter to Stage 6, are available as audio recordings. All Starters and many titles at Stages 1 to 4 are specially recommended for younger learners. Every Bookworm is illustrated, and Starters and Factfiles have full-color illustrations.

The OXFORD BOOKWORMS LIBRARY also offers extensive support. Each book contains an introduction to the story, notes about the author, a glossary, and activities. Additional resources include tests and worksheets, as well as answers for these and for the activities in the books. There is advice on running a class library, using audio recordings, and the many ways of using Oxford Bookworms in reading programs. Resource materials are available on the website <www.oup.com/bookworms>.

The *Oxford Bookworms Collection* is a series for advanced learners. It consists of volumes of short stories by well-known authors, both classic and modern. Texts are not abridged or adapted in any way, but carefully selected to be accessible to the advanced student.

You can find details and a full list of titles in the *Oxford Bookworms Library Catalog* and *Oxford English Language Teaching Catalogs*, and on the website <www.oup.com/bookworms>.

BOOKWORMS · TRUE STORIES · STAGE 1

The Elephant Man

TIM VICARY

He is not beautiful. His mother does not want him, and children run away from him. People laugh at him and call him "The Elephant Man."

Then someone speaks to him—and listens to him! At the age of 27, Joseph Merrick finds a friend for the first time in his life.

This is a true and tragic story. It is also a famous film.

BOOKWORMS · CLASSICS · STAGE 1

The Adventures of Tom Sawyer

MARK TWAIN

Retold by Nick Bullard

Tom Sawyer does not like school. He does not like work, and he never wants to get out of bed in the morning. But he likes swimming, fishing, and having adventures with his friends. And he has a lot of adventures. One night, he and his friend Huck Finn go to the graveyard to look for ghosts.

They don't see any ghosts that night. They see something worse than a ghost—much, much worse ...

The Wizard of Oz

L. FRANK BAUM

Retold by Rosemary Border

Dorothy lives in Kansas, but one day a cyclone blows Dorothy and her house to a strange country called Oz. There, Dorothy makes friends with the Scarecrow, the Tin Man, and the Cowardly Lion.

But she wants to go home to Kansas. Only one person can help her, and that is the country's famous Wizard. So Dorothy and her friends take the yellow brick road to the Emerald City, to find the Wizard of Oz ...

The Phantom of the Opera

JENNIFER BASSETT

It is 1880 in the Opera House in Paris. Everybody is talking about the Phantom of the Opera, the ghost that lives somewhere under the Opera House. The Phantom is a man in black clothes. He is a body without a head; he is a head without a body. He has a yellow face, he has no nose, and he has black holes for eyes. Everybody is afraid of the Phantom—the singers, the dancers, the directors, the stage workers ...

But who has actually seen him?

Huckleberry Finn

MARK TWAIN

Retold by Diane Mowat

Who wants to live in a house, wear clean clothes, be good, and go to school every day? Not young Huckleberry Finn, that's for sure.

So Huck runs away and is soon floating down the great Mississippi River on a raft. With him is Jim, a black slave who is also running away. But life is not always easy for the two friends.

And there's 300 dollars waiting for anyone who catches poor Jim …

Dracula

BRAM STOKER

Retold by Diane Mowat

In the mountains of Transylvania there stands a castle. It is the home of Count Dracula—a dark, lonely place. At night the wolves howl around the walls …

In the year 1875 Jonathan Harker comes from England to do business with the Count. But Jonathan does not feel comfortable at Castle Dracula. Strange things happen at night, and very soon he begins to feel afraid. And he is right to be afraid because Count Dracula is one of the Un-Dead—a vampire that drinks the blood of living people …